THE G.I. SERIES

- The War in Europe:
  From the Kasserine Pass to Berlin, 1942–1945

- Bluecoats:
  The U.S. Army in the West, 1848–1897

- Longknives:
  The U.S. Cavalry and Other Mounted Forces,
  1845–1942

- Billy Yank:
  The Uniform of the Union Army, 1861–1865

- Johnny Reb:
  The Uniform of the Confederate Army, 1861–1865

- The War in the Pacific:
  From Pearl Harbor to Okinawa, 1941–1945

- Over There!
  The American Soldier in World War I

- The U.S. Army Today:
  From the End of the Cold War to the Present Day

- The U.S. Marine Corps

- Patton's Third Army

- Redlegs:
  The U.S. Artillery from the Civil War to the
  Spanish-American War, 1861–1898

- Sound the Charge:
  The U.S. Cavalry in the American West, 1866–1916

- Fix Bayonets:
  The U.S. Infantry from the American Civil War
  to the Surrender of Japan

- Grunts:
  U.S. Infantry in Vietnam

Left: Cavalry trumpeters and musicians of the regimental band usually wore the 1855-pattern jacket with yellow lace worsted trim on the chest during the years immediately following the Civil War. The 1858-pattern hat was worn with the jacket, as was the forage cap. An example of a 'McDowell' pattern of this headgear, with its distinct sloping visor, can be seen on the chair to the trumpeter's right. With the exception of the company letter, no other insignia was prescribed with the cap, although a number of troopers added crossed sabers and regimental numerals, usually to the crown. (MJM)

THE G. I. SERIES

THE ILLUSTRATED HISTORY OF THE AMERICAN SOLDIER, HIS UNIFORM AND HIS EQUIPMENT

Sound the Charge
The U.S. Cavalry in the American West, 1866–1916

John P. Langellier

CHELSEA HOUSE PUBLISHERS

PHILADELPHIA

Library of Congress Cataloging-in-Publication Data
Langellier, J. Philip.
Sound the charge : the U.S. Cavalry in the American West. 1861–1916 /John P. Langellier.
   p.   cm.— (The G.I. series)
Originally published: London: Greenhill Books; Mechanicsburg, PA: Stackpole Books, © 1998, in series: G.I. series ; 12.
Includes index.
Summary: A history of the United States Cavalry in the American West throughout the nineteenth and twentieth centuries focusing on its uniforms and equipment.
ISBN 0-7910-5376-8 (hc)
1. United States. Army—Cavalry—History.   2. United States. Army—Uniforms—History—19th century.
3. United States Army—Uniforms—History—20th century.   4. United States. Army—Equipment—History—19th century.   5. United States. Army—Equipment—History—20th century.   6. West (U.S.)—History—1860–1890.   7. West (U.S.)—History—1890–1945.
[1. United States. Army—Cavalry—History.   2. United States. Army—Uniforms—History.   3. United States. Army—Equipment—History.   4. West (U.S.)—History.]   I. Title.   II. Series: G.I. series (Philadelphia, Pa.)
UE443. L36 1999
357'.1814'0973—dc21   99-13174
                    CIP

DEDICATION
This book is dedicated to Kurt Cox, friend and scholar.

ACKNOWLEDGEMENTS AND ABBREVIATIONS
The author wishes to thank the following individuals and staffs of the institutions listed below:

AHS	Arizona Historical Society
AMWH	Autry Museum of Western Heritage, Los Angeles, CA
BHW	B. William Henry
CBF	Casey Barthelmess Family
FAM	Frontier Army Museum, Fort Leavenworth, KS
FDNHS	Fort Davis National Historic Site, Fort Davis, TX
FUNHS	Fort Union National Historical Site
GH	Gordon Harrower
GM	Greg Martin
HP	Herb Peck, Jr.
JML	Joshua M. Landish
KSHS	Kansas State Historical Society, Topeka, KS
LBNB	Little Bighorn National Battlefield, Crow Agency, MT
LC	Library of Congress
MJM	Dr. Michael J. McAfee
NA	National Archives, Washington, DC
RBM	Reno Battlefield Museum, Garryowen, MT
RK	Robert L. Kotchian
SC	Seaver Center for Western History Research, Natural History Museum of Los Angeles
SI	Smithsonian Institution
TC	Tøjhusmuseet, Copenhagen, Denmark
UK	University of Kansas Libraries, Joseph Pennell Collection, Kansas Collection, Lawrence, KS
USAQM	U.S. Army Quartermaster Museum, Fort Lee, VA
USCM	U.S. Cavalry Museum, Fort Riley, KS
UTA	University of Texas, Austin
UTITC	University of Texas, Institute of Texan Culture, San Antonio, TX

Designed by DAG Publications Ltd
Designed by David Gibbons
Layout by Anthony A. Evans
Printed in Hong Kong

SOUND THE CHARGE
THE U.S. CAVALRY IN THE AMERICAN WEST, 1861–1916

In 1865 a victorious Yankee army began to disband. No longer needed to fight a life-and-death struggle to preserve the Union, most of the men who wore the blue now put aside their uniforms and returned to civilian pursuits.

Not all of these veterans, however, were to follow this course. The nation still needed a force to occupy the defeated South, as radical Republicans used the military as a sword to enforce the policies of Reconstruction. In the West, ever-growing numbers of settlers, miners, and others flowed into the region between the Mississippi River and the Pacific Ocean in search of land, riches, or scores of other inducements both real and imagined. Their presence heightened tensions with the first inhabitants of the deserts, mountains, and plains – people referred to as 'Indians' by those who came in a steady stream from the East and elsewhere. The borders between Canada and the United States, and the sometimes volatile line separating Mexico from its northern neighbor, likewise required troops, especially during the period of unrest when the Austrian archduke Maximilian ruled as Emperor of Mexico.

Recognizing these many military needs, the U.S. Congress voted to establish a standing army of more than 50,000 men, triple the antebellum strength authorized before events at Fort Sumter propelled the nation into four years of internecine conflict. As part of this 1866 organization, approximately one-fifth of the total force would be made up of ten regiments of cavalry, including two of black enlisted men, some of whom had served the Union in the late war, and many others who had been held in slavery. Others who came into the service had been Confederates, but now accepted the stars and stripes as 'Galvanized Yankees.' Moreover, thousands of people who had arrived in the United States as part of a great movement from Europe, fleeing famine, oppression, and a litany of other problems, would see the U.S. cavalry as an opportunity worth pursuing.

Over the next three decades many of these horse soldiers, both black and white, saw their share of hard campaigning. On occasion they clashed with the 'finest light cavalry in the world,' the hard-riding Plains tribes that made banner headlines in the press of the day, especially during the summer of 1876 when they devastated George Armstrong Custer's five troops at the Little Bighorn.

In the Southwest, Apache, Comanche, and Kiowa all battled bravely to halt the incursion of westward expansion. So, too, did the Modoc, who held-out against superior odds in their extraordinary lava-bed stronghold (one not of man's making, but provided by nature). The Nez Perce also made a momentous exodus, attempting to evade pursuing cavalry and infantry in a desperate attempt to cross into the 'Queen Mother Land' – Canada – where they hoped to gain sanctuary.

From time to time, bandits, Mexican revolutionaries, and Irish Fenians who sought to wrest Canada from Britain, had to be pursued and subdued as well. Keeping guard over expanding railroads and telegraph lines, along with stage routes and overland trails, meant many cavalrymen were in the saddle during bitter cold and searing heat. Even protecting the newly established national parks in the West from poachers and others fell to their lot. For the most part, however, the average trooper of the 1860s through 1890s seldom saw an enemy in combat.

Indeed, under-strength units experienced considerable difficulty in their field operations in often harsh terrain. During the three decades immediately following the Civil War, the regimental strength rarely reached the authorized four officers, fifteen non-commissioned officers, and seventy-two privates per company. There were to be twelve such companies per regiment, commanded by a colonel and his seven-man regimental staff of fellow officers, along with six enlisted men, a surgeon and a pair of assistant surgeons. Further, the Ninth and Tenth Cavalry Regiments also had a chaplain assigned to each headquarters as both spiritual leader and educational director; apparently, these units contained many illiterate men who wanted to learn to read and write.

Besides this prescribed table of organization, a Congressional Act of 28 July 1866 allowed for a corps of Indian scouts, with a total army-wide strength of 1,000. Commanders could enlist such auxiliaries, who often came from groups that had traditional enmity toward the people being pursued, such as in the case of the Crow who rode with Custer against the Sioux and Northern Cheyenne in the 1876 summer campaign. In other instances, however, one band from the same nation was pitted against another group of their kinsmen, such as in the Apache campaigns. As one officer of the time phrased it, 'it takes diamond dust to polish a diamond.' In all cases, the scouts were to be signed on for six-month periods through the Quartermaster's Department. These men became important in bringing an end to the so-called Indian Wars.

The scouts and cavalrymen were scattered among ninety-two posts in the mid-1860s through the 1870s, all in the West. By 1882 that number had been consolidated to fifty garrisons, with most troopers being stationed in the Departments of the Missouri and Texas.

Being so dispersed, the companies gained a certain level of competence in irregular warfare against the highly mobile American Indians, and actually developed tactics that allowed them to fight either on horseback or on foot, once they had closed with their foe. On the other hand, this type of operation did not provide for adequate training or experience in the event of meeting a more conventional enemy face-to-face.

Realizing that this situation could prove disastrous should another war erupt against a foreign power, the army began to establish schools that would provide a foundation for such a contingency. In 1881 the School of Application for Infantry and Cavalry opened at Fort Leavenworth, Kansas, followed a half dozen years later by plans to create a school at Fort Riley, Kansas which focused on the training of enlisted cavalrymen and light artillerymen.

Students were taught the intricacies of unit maneuvers that went beyond the troop (a term officially adopted in 1883 as universal for a cavalry company, although from the 1860s used interchangeably with the term company), and in some instances were offered the opportunity to operate in tandem with field artillery or infantry. The same standardized tactics that had been adopted by the infantry in 1867, based on a system developed by Brevet Major General Emory Upton, were adapted for the cavalry in 1873, so that mounted and dismounted elements could work from a unified formation concept.

For cavalry, this meant a squadron consisted of from two to four troops. In turn, the troops were divided into two, three, or four platoons, depending on the number of men available, to allow for the basic building block of the organization – sets of fours. The fours were so rudimentary as to be reflected in horse equipment, with each man's bridle having hardware and a strap to allow for the linking together of four horses, thereby permitting three men to dismount and fight on foot, while their fourth member served as 'the horse-holder' during an engagement. Such a tactic had an obvious drawback, however, in that it effectively reduced the combat force by a quarter. Nevertheless, this was the accepted standard for many years.

While the cavalry manual was codified for more than a generation, change did occur in other areas. For one thing, the gradual reduction of combat between the military and American Indians led to the closure of many posts in the West, and the consolidation of the cavalry to some thirty-one garrisons, all of which were beyond the Mississippi, except for squadrons at Fort Ethan Allen, Vermont and Fort Myer, Virginia.

The number of troops assigned to a regiment was also reduced. In 1890 Troops L and M were disbanded and the former practice of having up to 100 enlisted men per troop was halted. Thereafter, only forty-four privates were to make up a troop. These economy measures indicated the near completion of the horse soldiers' mission as an Indian-fighting force.

By the following year, however, an experiment that attempted to integrate certain Indian groups into the Regular Army gave rise to the resurrection of Troop L in the First through Eighth Cavalry Regiments. This short-lived attempt to employ the warrior experience of the Crow, Cheyenne, Sioux, and others met with mixed success, ending slightly later in the decade with the abandonment of the project and the discontinuance of Troop Ls once more.

Even as Indian troopers made their brief appearance in uniform, a new magazine weapon was introduced to replace the old single-shot black powder .45-caliber Springfield 'trapdoor' carbine. By 1896 the cavalry began to follow in the footsteps of the infantry, by officially adopting the smokeless powder .30-caliber Krag-Jörgensen carbines as their new arm. Not until 1898, however, did all Regular Army troopers receive this weapon.

Final issue of the Krag essentially coincided with the outbreak of war in Cuba. Soon cavalrymen from across the country, along with their comrades in the infantry and artillery, and volunteers from around the nation, assembled in preparation to ship overseas against the Spanish. The Spanish-American War brought a reinstatement of Troops L and M to all the Regular Army cavalry regiments, as well as an increase in the strength of each troop by a lieutenant, a sergeant, four corporals, and an additional thirty-four privates over the peacetime organization. Now a troop was to be 104 men strong, and a regiment to total 1,262 officers and troopers.

Thousands of men from the First, Third, Sixth, Ninth, and Tenth Cavalry Regiments, along with a squadron of the Second Cavalry, shipped to Cuba for a brief, brisk campaign, albeit fighting chiefly on foot. Leaving behind sabers and most of their mounts, they faced the Mausers of the Spaniards at places such as La Guasima and San Juan Hill, although in the latter engagement their success was overshadowed by the popular press coverage of Theodore Roosevelt and his 'Rough Riders,' the men of the First U.S. Volunteer Cavalry.

The Second Cavalry's squadron did have horses in Cuba, however, as did one of the troops of that regiment who were sent to Puerto Rico in 1898. The next year the Fourth Cavalry followed suit with men and mounts being the first of nine Regular Army cavalry regiments to be assigned to the Philippines between 1899 and 1901, after Spain had surrendered this former possession.

Two other outfits were raised for duty in the Philippines, including the Eleventh U.S. States Volunteer Cavalry, whose ranks were filled in the main by U.S. citizens living in the islands. They were joined by a squadron of Filipinos, and both organizations were active until disbandment on 2 July 1901. Just prior to these two units standing down, Congress again permitted an increase in the U.S. Army, including the creation of the Eleventh through Fifteenth U.S. Cavalry Regiments. Personnel strength was increased in all of the cavalry regiments, with the addition of another captain, three second lieutenants, a commissary sergeant, two color sergeants, and a chaplain, along with a provision for the president to permit 164 enlisted men per troop at his discretion rather than the 100 men allowed previously.

While many of these regiments continued serving in the American West, for the most part along the border with Mexico, substantial numbers of troopers were quartered in the Philippines, Hawaii, Panama, and even in China. There, the Sixth Cavalry formed part of the relief expedition to Peking, during the Boxer Rebellion in 1900.

Now operating as part of an international power, the U.S. Cavalry found itself deployed in diverse areas around the globe. Its leadership no longer saw the horse soldiers' function as a police force in the West, but instead had fixed upon an image along European lines. As such, the cavalry revived tactics from the mid-nineteenth century, and also experimented with a number of new modes of organization. As one example, from 1911 through 1912, the twelve troops of each regiment were reduced to six by combining pairs of companies; theoretically, this would result in a more compact unit that would provide easier command and control in combat. While marksmanship and dismounted drill were not abandoned during this transitional time, additional emphasis was given to mounted training, improved horse flesh, and a return to sabers as a primary weapon.

These various experiments, including a new trial service regulation for cavalry from 1914 to 1916, received less than enthusiastic support from commanders in the field. By 1916 a return to the former tactics and organizational structure resulted, although several elements of the new experimental drill and regulations were incorporated with the old system.

On 6 March of that year a raid by Mexican bandits on Columbus, New Mexico provoked the mobilization of the cavalry, as well as other Regular Army and National Guard elements. Soon olive drab-clad troops crossed into Mexico, chiefly to corner Francisco 'Pancho' Villa, the accused perpetrator of the Columbus raid and arch villain in the eyes of President Woodrow Wilson's government. Pursuit of such an elusive guerrilla quarry in a foreign land, however, proved difficult. Neither the Mexican government, nor the local populace cooperated with the hard-riding *Gringos* who came on the 'Punitive Expedition.' Nonetheless, despite many hardships, the American cavalrymen demonstrated their grit in what was the last major action conducted by U.S. horse soldiers. In one instance, for example, on 29 March 1916, 400 men of the Seventh Cavalry rode for seventeen hours during a twenty-four hour period. At the end of this gruelling ride, they made a surprise attack against an estimated 500 Villistas camped at Guerrero.

While not an overwhelming success, the Punitive Expedition at least demonstrated the cavalry's state of readiness, and also allowed innovations, including the motor transport of supplies and the employment of machine guns, to be tested under combat conditions. These innovations would soon be vital when the United States turned its eyes from neighboring Mexico to a new challenge, the trenches of France where the First World War drew the Yanks into the fray in 1917. When the American Expeditionary Force threw its hat into the ring and headed 'over there', its leader would be none other than an experienced cavalryman who had gained fame and even his nickname, 'Black Jack' (because of his early service as a company grade officer with the Tenth Cavalry, one of the regiments of black troopers), when he rode in the forefront of the Punitive Expedition: General John J. Pershing.

Despite Pershing's lofty rise to command the AEF, World War I spelled the end of the horse cavalry as a major military arm, although the last bugle call of 'Boots and Saddles' was decades in the future. Even though mechanization would remove the military need for the horse in the 20th century, the tradition of trooper and mount remain strong both in those U.S. Army units that continue to be designated by the name cavalry, and in popular images of art, fiction, movies, and television that conjure up vivid images when 'Sound the Charge!' is heard.

FOR FURTHER READING

Cox, Kurt Hamilton and Langellier, John P., *Longknives: The U.S. Cavalry and Other Mounted Forces, 1845–1942*. London: Greenhill Books, 1996.

Dunlay, Thomas W., *Wolves for the Blue Soldiers: Indian Scouts and Auxiliaries with the United States Army, 1860–90*. Lincoln: University of Nebraska Press, 1982.

Leckie, William H., *The Buffalo Soldiers: A Narrative of the Negro Cavalry in the West*. Norman: University of Oklahoma Press, 1967.

Stubbs, Mary Lee and Connor, Stanley Russell., *Armor Cavalry Part 1: Regular Army and Army Reserve*. Washington, DC: Office of the Chief of Military History, 1960.

Urwin, Gregory J.W., *The United States Cavalry: An Illustrated History*. Poole: Blandford Press, 1983.

Left: Civil War stocks were used to clothe horse soldiers for many years after the North and South ceased fighting. The dark blue wool jacket with yellow worsted tape remained the official dress uniform for cavalrymen from 1861 through 1872, as seen here for a trumpeter of cavalry. The hat is not looped on the right side, however, as was regulation. (USAQM)

Below: The 1858-pattern cavalry enlisted hat was to bear stamped sheet brass crossed sabers, a company letter, a regimental numeral, worsted yellow hat cords with tassel ends, and a black ostrich feather. The right side of the brim was to be held against the side by means of a stamped sheet brass Arms of the United States device. (JML)

Left: Cavalry officers wore a similar 1858-pattern hat, but all insignia was to be embroidered in gold and silver, while the cords were to be gold and black, terminating in acorns. Company grade officers (lieutenants through captains) were to have two black ostrich feathers affixed to the left side, and field grade officers (majors through colonels) were to have three. (JML)

Bottom left and right: Front and rear view of the enlisted cavalry jacket first issued in 1855, and worn until the early 1870s. (WYO)

Above: The 1851-pattern mounted overcoat remained in service throughout the early 1870s. (TC)

Left: An official U.S. Army Quartermaster photograph shows the mounted overcoat in combination with the forage cap that was commonly seen during the American Civil War. (USAQM)

Above left: This pattern of the long single-breasted white canvas stable frock closed with three buttons. Adopted as early as the 1850s, these garments were issued to mounted troops to keep their more expensive wool uniforms from being soiled. The canvas could also be washed easily, a necessary requirement because the color undoubtedly showed the dirt attendant with grooming horses, cleaning stalls, and other chores associated with maintaining a mount. Overalls of this pattern were also worn under the stable frock by cavalry and light artillery troops from 1872. (USAQM)

Above right: The shade of facing material designating cavalry was changed to a darker hue in 1887, as the lighter version tended to fade after exposure to the sun and elements. This is a first sergeant in the dress uniform prescribed in that year and which remained regulation until 1903. The single service stripe above the cuff flash indicates one completed enlistment. (RBM)

Left: A variant of the officers' 1872-pattern cavalry shoulder knots, in this case for a captain of the Second U.S. Cavalry. Usually the knots were made with gold wire-covered cords, rather than cords and embroidery. (WSM)

Right: A new enlisted blouse was adopted in 1884 with three slash pockets, although photographic evidence indicates that this garment was not worn widely. The insignia is that of a farrier. (SI)

Cavallerist.   Brigade-General.   Infanterie-Offizier.   Generalstabs-Offizier.   Artillerie-Offizier.   Cavallerie-Offizier.

Above: The trooper on the far left is a sergeant of cavalry, as indicated by the three chevrons on his post-1884 jacket or blouse, and the 1-inch stripes of yellow facing material on the outer trouser seams. The forage cap is the 1872-pattern, which by the period depicted here (1885–92) had stamped sheet brass crossed sabers with the regimental number above, and troop letter below. The officers in this uniform (originally depicted in a late 19th-century German-language publication) all appear in the garrison and field uniform of the same era as the sergeant. (LC)

Above: A cavalry officer reports to a brigadier general (George Crook) in the full dress uniform of the 1887–1902 period. The cords for officers were gold, rather than the yellow worsted for enlisted men. Plumes for officers were to be buffalo or yak hair. The officers in the background (left to right) are cavalry, light artillery, staff, and a field grade infantry officer. (RBM)

Left: A cavalry troop on patrol in the mid-1880s through early 1890s. Horses were color matched by troop in most instances, although the trumpeters usually rode lighter colored mounts. (WCC)

Right: The cavalry officer and enlisted man wearing the 1887 through 1902 dress uniform contrast with the khaki clad outfit adopted in 1898 for wear in Cuba, Puerto Rico, and the Philippines during the Spanish-American War. (WCC)

Right: The 1902 uniform changes continued with the use of a stand collar jacket with black mohair trim, as seen in the case of the cavalry officer in the center of this Henry A. Ogden illustration. A cavalry trumpeter in the 1902-pattern enlisted dress uniform appears in the left background. (WCC)

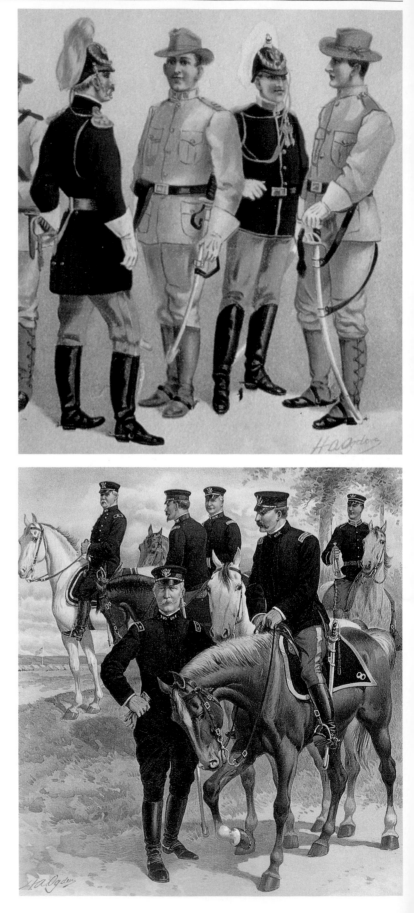

Left: After the Civil War most cavalrymen served in the American West. A few troopers were posted elsewhere, however. This corporal, stationed at the United States Military Academy, has custom chevrons in yellow worsted lace on his 1855-pattern jacket, and has acquired a chasseur-style forage cap, on the front of which he has placed a small privately purchased saber insignia. The brass fittings sewn to his jacket to hold the shoulder scales in place are evident, too. Corporals' trousers were to have a ½-inch yellow worsted stripe sewn to each outer seam. (MJM)

Right: A sergeant at the Military Academy during the mid to late 1860s wears the standard 1½-inch worsted yellow stripes on his trousers, although there is no evidence of chevrons on the jacket. This is one of several departures from regulations, as are his gauntlets, which are either photographer's props or privately purchased, because none were issued during this period. The forage cap is the standard issue item, with tall crown. (MJM)

Above left: The trooper seated in the front row center clearly exhibits the reinforcing that was part of trouser construction for mounted troops. Sky-blue kersey cloth of the same color and material of the trousers themselves was sewn from the seat to the inside of the thighs and calves, all the way to the ankles to make the trousers more resilient to saddle wear. (MJM)

Above: The reinforcement of the saddling piece on this buffalo soldier who posed in the late 1860s or early 1870s from Company M, Tenth U.S. Cavalry, is clear. There are buttons at the center of the waist to close the trousers, and buttons for suspenders (braces) on either side at the waist. The shirt is possibly a privately purchased garment. (HP)

Left: Three sergeants from the cavalry detachment serving at West Point, *c.* 1870, illustrate the continuance of Civil War issue uniforms, including the four-button sack coat and the twelve-button mounted jacket. The collar of the non-commissioned officer on the left appears to be lower than the regulation pattern. (MJM)

Right: An unidentified cavalry officer in the 1851-pattern cloak coat that was regulation until 1872. The low-crowned forage cap is the chasseur type favored by many officers and some enlisted men during the Civil War. (MJM)

Left: This *c.* 1870 cavalryman had his four-button sack coat tailored and an exterior breast pocket added. His cap also appears to be privately purchased, being somewhat more dapper than the issue version. (MJM)

Left: Captain George Yates of the Seventh Cavalry has obtained a civilian jacket with dark frogs and fleece-lined lapels and collar, plus pockets. This was a functional winter field garment worn instead of the regulation frock coat or four-button sack coat. Once more, gauntlets and high boots were selected for field use, while the jaunty, but less practical, chasseur forage cap tops off this outfit of the late 1860s through early 1870s. The ⅛-inch yellow welt for officers can be discerned on his trousers. (LBNB)

Above: The Seventh Cavalry's lieutenant colonel, George A. Custer, fancied himself a frontiersman and adopted the look of a scout in this 1872 portrait, complete with broad brimmed hat and buckskin outfit. One of the few military concessions are the cavalry officers' buttons on the fringed jacket. The red scarf was a trademark of Custer's outfit that he continued from his Civil War service. (RBM)

Above: The 1851-pattern sky-blue kersey mounted over-coat was issued until the 1870s. Here a trooper at Fort Bridger, Wyoming Territory is made to mount the 'moral suasion horse' with a heavy wooden saber, as a punishment for some infraction. (WYO)

Right: Officers also could obtain the 1872-pattern folding hat, often with tape binding on the brim, as this cavalry officer has done. He wears the 1872-pattern officers' jacket with five black mohair trefoils at the end of braid trimming the chest. The same material edged the collar and skirts of the coat, and ornamented its back as well as the cuffs. Shoulder straps, which for some unexplained reason are absent here, were used to designate rank. He holds the M1859 light cavalry saber. (MJM)

The 1872-pattern officers' jacket could be worn with the 1872-pattern officers' forage cap. In this *c.* 1873 portrait, Second Lieutenant A. H. Russell, Third U.S. Cavalry, also wears the correct shoulder straps of his rank with yellow centers. (RBM)

Wᵐ O Taylor, Troop M 7ᵗ Cav- 1872.- 1877. Taken about 1875; at Fort Rice, North Dakota.

one of Major Renos command at the battle of the "Little Big Horn" June 25ᵗ 26ᵗ 1876.

Above: Private William O. Tayler of the Seventh U.S. Cavalry sat for the photographer in the 1872-pattern cavalry enlisted dress coat and an 1872-pattern forage cap. All facings were to be yellow. A helmet was prescribed with this coat, however, for enlisted men. (GM)

Left: The enlisted 1872-pattern cavalry dress helmet had yellow cords and a yellow horsetail plume to match the trim of the coat. The collar was to display a pair of stamped sheet brass regimental numbers, one on each side, in this instance for the Seventh U.S. Cavalry. (MJM)

Above: Enlisted helmet cords were made in one piece and attached to the helmet, but some enlisted men cut the cords to make it easier to remove this rather cumbersome head-piece when not in use. (BHW)

Above right: The pronounced rear visor of Private John S. Ogden's 1872-pattern dress helmet is evident in this portrait, taken while he was with Company E, Seventh U.S.

Cavalry at Fort Lincoln, Dakota Territory. Later, he was promoted to sergeant, a rank he held when he was killed at the Little Bighorn. (RBM)

Below: Not long after the battle at the Little Bighorn in June 1876, men of Company B, Seventh U.S. Cavalry, gathered for a group portrait in their 1872 dress uniforms which remained regulation until 1881, when a new helmet was adopted. (RBM)

Right: First Lieutenant Peter Boehm wears the company grade uniform prescribed for dress purposes in 1872, including the top-heavy helmet with steep rear visor. The plume is yellow horsehair, and the cords on the helmet and his chest are of metallic gold thread. The gilt eagle device on the front of the helmet was to bear a silver number to indicate the regiment. The shoulder knots have yellow centers with a silver embroidered '4' flanked by single silver bars on each side of the numbers to indicate rank. The saber is a non-regulation edged weapon characteristic of Civil War presentation pieces. Perhaps this sword was a gift from associates in recognition of his valor during the Civil War battle at Dinwiddie Courthouse, Virginia. (NA)

Left: Second Lieutenant H. G. Squires holds an 1872-pattern helmet with the foot of the plume socket set in a cruciform manner (with the feet at the front and back rather than at angles as was the norm), a variation attributed to military outfitter Baker & McKenney of New York. The sleeves lack gold lace, this ornamentation being discontinued on officers' coats in 1880. (JML)

Left: A new field blouse was adopted in 1872 for enlisted men with the collar, cuffs, and yoke piped in yellow cord. This pleated blouse is worn by Private Howard Weaver, Troop A, Seventh Cavalry, along with the 1872-pattern folding campaign hat. Neither item was particularly popular with the troops. (GM)

Right: Privates Timothy Donnelly (right) and George Walker (left) were photographed around 1875 in the 1872-pattern enlisted forage cap without insignia. They wear the 1861-pattern blue kersey mounted trousers, to which Donnelly has added a belt for support, despite the fact that there are no belt loops. He has also tied a small bandanna about the neck over his 1874-pattern gray flannel shirt. These men were troopers in the Seventh U.S. Cavalry. (RBM)

Left: The unpopular 1872-pattern hat and blouse were replaced in the mid-1870s. William O. Tyler of the Seventh U.S. Cavalry wears the 1874-pattern five-button blouse that replaced the 1872-pattern pleated blouse. His hat may be the 1876-pattern campaign hat, or possibly a civilian slouch hat that he has fitted out with stamped brass crossed sabers and regimental numeral, along with the 1858-pattern yellow worsted hat cords. The addition of such items to the hat, although not unknown, tended to be rather limited in practice. (GM)

Below: An assortment of uniform items, both issue and non-issue, are worn by these Sixth U.S. Cavalry troopers in Arizona Territory at Fort Grant in 1883. Most wear the 1874-pattern enlisted blouse with collars and cuffs piped in yellow. The man on the far right of the rear row, however, has retained the 1872-pattern nine-button pleated blouse with the yoke, collar, and cuffs piped in yellow. The soldier at the far left has unhooked the 1872-pattern folding hat which he has adorned with a yellow hat cord and 1872-pattern cavalry brass sabers. These were not commonly used on headgear, as indicated by their absence on all the other hats here. The man seated on the left has on an oil cloth cover for his 1872-pattern forage cap, while all the other men have obtained civilian headgear not unlike that worn by cowhands of the region. Finally, an 1881-pattern piped blue shirt is worn by the man seated second from right, indicated by the yellow piping which trims the front. (AHS)

This group of Sixth Cavalry troops in New Mexico Territory wear several variations of uniform items, including the 1876-pattern black campaign hat and what is possibly an 1874-pattern blouse with the cord removed per orders in 1884 to discontinue trim on the enlisted field jacket. One trooper standing to the rear left wears the 1883-pattern shirt with his cartridges for his 'forage gun,' tucked in the fly. The young scout in the center wears what appears to be a blue shirt of the type made up in the summer of 1875 from lightweight blouse material. The man seated on the left has the post 1883-pattern blouse and an 1876-pattern muskrat cap. The man seated on the right has donned an 1877 experimental collarless gray shirt and a pair of M1876 boots covered by arctic overshoes. The rest of the men also wear M1876 boots. The trooper seated on the right seems to have obtained a custom leather 'saddler's' belt for his shotgun ammunition, while the scout and the soldier in the right background use early Mills belts with two-piece cast buckles for their .45 caliber Spring carbine ammunition. (CBF)

Below: Captain M. M. Maxon in the 1881 through 1903 company grade cavalry officers' uniform. The numeral on his gilt helmet plate is a silver '10' to indicate his regiment. The saber is the M1872 for cavalry officers. (FDNHS)

Left: Captain Maxon's 1881-pattern dress helmet with gold breast cord. (FDNHS)

Left: Lieutenant Daniel H. Boughton, Third U.S. Cavalry, wears the 1872-pattern officers' forage cap with the gold embroidered crossed sabers device surmounted by a silver embroidered '3.' The gold cord cap strap is of the pattern adopted by General Order No. 102, 26 December 1883, which sanctioned an item already worn unofficially by officers instead of the regulation leather strap. He wears the handsome 1885-pattern dark blue Ulster officers' overcoat as well. (FAM)

Above: Cavalry dress parade at Fort Riley, Kansas. Each troop guidon bearer carries the 1885-pattern guidon. All wear the 1887 through 1903 dress uniform. (UK)

Left: Cavalry private in the 1881 through 1884 dress uniform. The facings, cords, and plume are yellow. (FUNHS)

Right: Private C. M. Scaten wears the 1872-pattern cavalry enlisted dress coat without regimental numerals, which were discontinued as of 1884. (FAM)

Left: Private J. A. Morrow, Troop M, Sixth U.S. Cavalry, wears marksmanship devices of the mid-1880s on the collar of his five-button blouse, which is of the pattern commonly issued from the mid-1880s until the turn of the century. The 1872-pattern forage cap bears the proper insignia prescribed in the 1870s. Vests (waistcoats) and cravats were permitted by this period as well, but had to be purchased by the soldier rather than being issue items. Privates were paid only $13 per month, and these additional clothing items were probably viewed as extravagant by some men. (FAM)

Right: An unidentified cavalry trooper in the 1881-pattern enlisted helmet (although the plume is possibly an officers' or non-regulation one) and the 1885-pattern full dress coat. The 1885-pattern dress coat had facing material covering the entire collar rather then just a welt around the top and bottom of the collar, and 4-inch patches on either side. (MJM)

Below: Officers of the Seventh U.S. Cavalry at Wounded Knee, South Dakota in 1890 appear in a wide variety of headgear, ranging from the 1883-pattern to the 1889-pattern campaign hat, civilian slouch hats, issue muskrat hats, privately-purchased fur caps, and the 1872-pattern forage cap The officer seated third from left in the front row wears the 1883-pattern campaign hat. Almost all the officers wear the 1875-pattern officers' five-button blouse with shoulder straps. Yellow 1½inch stripes are visible on many of the officers' light blue trousers. (USCM)

Left: Regimental adjutants wore an aiguillette under the right shoulder knot of their full dress uniform, as demonstrated by Second Lieutenant Scott of the First U.S. Cavalry in this 1895 photo. (UK)

Below left: Clarence Pole played the clarinet with the Sixth U.S. Cavalry band at Fort Wingate, New Mexico Territory. He wears the 1885-pattern cavalry musicians' dress coat with worsted shoulder knots, and attached cords adopted in that year for bandsmen. (BWH)

Below: John Jefferson, a former member of the Seminole Negro Scouts, became a trumpeter with Troop D, Tenth U.S. Cavalry. He wears the regulation double ½-inch yellow leg stripes prescribed for musicians and trumpeters in 1883, and a sharpshooters' pin that was instituted in 1885. The cap is the 1895-pattern enlisted forage cap with a one-piece screwback insignia. (Courtesy Mrs John Jefferson, UTITC)

Above: By the 1890s, bandsmen continued to have options in terms of their uniform, as seen here for the musicians of the Third U.S. Cavalry, stationed at Jefferson Barracks, Missouri in the mid- to late 1890s. All wear the worsted dark yellow shoulder knots sanctioned in 1885, but instead of the standard herringbone on the chests of their 1885-pattern coats, they have a triple row of buttons. The drummer in the front row center did double-duty as indicated by his chevrons with a leather knife above, this being the device for a saddler sergeant. The double ½-inch yellow leg stripes, which were authorized in 1883 but worn unofficially prior to that time, are not seen here. Instead, they wear 1-inch leg stripes of the type specified for sergeants. (NA)

Right: Crow scouts had ridden with the Seventh Cavalry to the Little Bighorn. A generation later, in the early 1890s, several members of the Crow nation joined Troop L, First U.S. Cavalry as troopers. This is one of that group at Fort Custer, Montana, complete with saber, 1872-pattern forage cap, and the cavalry's garrison uniform of the early 1890s. (NA)

Above: Lieutenant Little William Brown's command, Troop C, First U.S. Cavalry, at San Carlos Apache Reservation, Arizona Territory in the field uniform of the late Victorian era. Carbines are the relatively late model .45 caliber Springfield 'trapdoors' with removable hoods over the front sights. The guidon is the 1885-pattern. Note also the brown canvas leggings that began to be issued in the late 1880s as an alternative to boots. (NA)

Left: Private C. A. Wolford of the First Cavalry on his horse 'Buttons' carries his carbine in a leather carbine boot suspended from an M1885 carbine sling with snap. He has drawn his saber despite the fact that this weapon was of little use in the field against Indian groups of the era. (NA)

Right: Private William E. Riley strikes a nonchalant stance in the cavalry field uniform typical of the late 1880s through the turn of the century. The pistol is the .45 caliber Colt 'single-action' rather than the 'double-action' .38 caliber revolver that began to be issued earlier in the decade on a gradual replacement basis for the larger bore handgun. (NA)

Below: Troop E, First U.S. Cavalry, at Fort Washakie, Wyoming wear the 1884-pattern stable uniforms with 1889-pattern campaign hat while training their mounts to lie down on command. This picture was taken in 1899, although the basic uniform is that adopted a decade earlier. (NA)

Opposite page, top: The cavalry school at Fort Riley, Kansas was established in the 1890s, in an effort to train troops for a potential war with a European power or conventional enemy. This massive indoor riding hall was constructed to ensure that equitation practice could be carried out whatever the season or weather. (UK)

Opposite page, bottom: Not all soldiers' duties were on the parade ground where 'spit and polish' was the order of the day, as men serving at one of Fort Riley's mess halls of the mid-1890s demonstrate. (UK)

Above: Other assignments requiring specialized clothing included blacksmithing. The blacksmith at left center wears khaki trousers and what may be the 1902-pattern light blue cotton-chambray shirt. (UK)

Right: A sergeant from Troop D, Third U.S. Cavalry, proudly poses with his 1872-pattern forage cap, which tops off the garrison uniform of the mid- to late 1880s. From 1872, sergeants were to have 1-inch stripes on the outer seams of their trousers in yellow facing material. Also note the sergeant's chevrons on the blouse of the type worn from the mid-1880s through early 1900s for garrison duty and campaigns. The device on his chest is a marksmanship pin of the type adopted in 1885. (FSHM)

Left: Arrayed in a variety of regulation and non-regulation items, these men of Troop G, Second U.S. Cavalry, were captured by photographer Joseph Pennell in 1897. Four of them wear 1889-pattern unbleached cotton duck stable overalls, and three have 1888-pattern mounted sky-blue kersey reinforced trousers. The dark blue flannel shirts are 1883-pattern, the remainder of the shirts being canton undershirts. The soldier on the far left, however, wears what seems to be a privately purchased civilian white shirt instead of a regulation item. The saddles are M1885 McClellans. (UK)

Above: Troopers from Fort Riley's school for cavalrymen prepare for a parade in nearby Junction City, Kansas in their 1880-pattern white summer helmets. (UK)

Below: Smartly dressed officers and men of Troop A, Fourteenth Cavalry, turn out in the garrison uniform of the 1895 through 1903 era, with dark blue blouses, sky-blue trousers, and 1895-pattern forage caps. (UK)

Above: Troop A, Second U.S. Cavalry, the majority of whom wear their stable uniforms of white canvas or unbleached drilling. (UK)

Below: Men of Troop A, Fifth U.S. Cavalry stand at 'parade rest' without their carbines. They wear the sky-blue kersey overcoat of the type adopted in the 1880s, and worn until the turn of the century with only minor modifications. All the troopers have removed the detachable capes of matching sky-blue with yellow linings for this *c.* 1895 photograph. Chevrons, as seen here, were to be worn on greatcoats with points down positioned between the elbows and cuffs according to an 1883 general order. In this way, the rank would not be obscured by the cape, when that portion of the coat was worn. (USCM)

Right: A cavalry officer wears the stand collar mohair blouse which was adopted in 1895 and continued in use into the 20th century. The block style 'U.S.' insignia and crossed sabers with regimental numbers were to be positioned on the collar. These could be gilt metal or embroidered in gold. There was also a similar white version of this jacket. The M1889 officer's boots are also evident, as is the M1872 saber for cavalry officers. An M1874 curb bridle with 'Shoemaker' bit and the M1885 McClellan saddle and saddle bags of the same model are other major elements of the horse equipment. (NA)

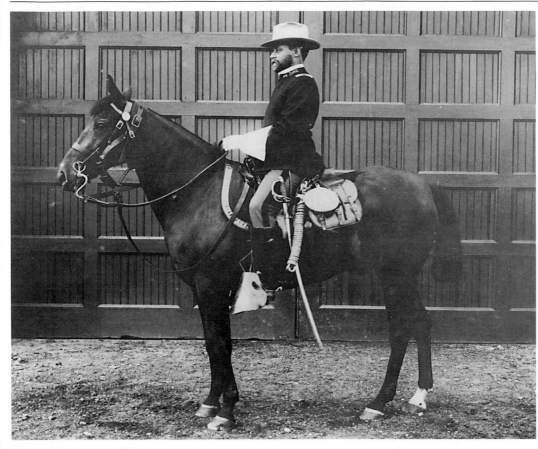

Below: Lightweight white canvas or unbleached drilling three-button stable frocks could be traced back to before the Civil War. In 1872, trousers were added to the outfit. Seven years later, specifications called for the coat to have a stand collar to help prevent dirt getting down the wearer's neck. The collar could be turned down as well. These men of Troop A, Second U.S. Cavalry, wear the stable frock with the 1889-pattern campaign hat. The M1885 watering bridle with bit is also evident. (AMWH)

Left: Lieutenant George M. Russell of the Fourteenth Cavalry. His mount has the M1892 bit. The saddle cloth is dark blue edged in yellow leather and the regimental numeral is also of leather. Only officers were permitted this design of saddle cloth. The slash at the hip of the 1895-pattern officers' jacket can be seen, along with the black buttons that could be used to close the opening when dismounted. (UK)

Right: In the 1880s brown canvas leggings gradually began to replace high top boots. This 1897 photo of Private Evans of Troop A, Second U.S. Cavalry at Fort Riley, Kansas, shows what appear to be 1886-pattern (or perhaps the 1896-pattern) goat-skin gauntlets. He holds the .30 caliber Krag-Jörgensen carbine and wears his 1889-pattern campaign hat at a tilt. The device on his collar is not regulation. (UK)

Left: A group of cavalry recruits at Fort Riley, Kansas lounge in front of their barracks in 1896. The two men on the left wear 1889-pattern campaign hats, while another comrade appears in the 1880-pattern cork summer helmet covered with white duck. The remainder of the men wear the 1895-pattern enlisted forage cap. Both 1883-pattern shirts and 1884-pattern five-button blouses are evident. All but one of the men wears sky-blue mounted reinforced trousers, the exception being the soldier in the 1888-pattern white duck trousers. Suspenders (braces) were to be invisible, so three of the group wear the M1885 saber belt to help keep their trousers in place, although no belt loops were provided during this period. (UK)

Left: A private of Troop L, Fifth U.S. Cavalry in the 1895-pattern forage cap with screw-back insignia. He holds the .30 caliber Krag carbine that was adopted for the cavalry in 1896 and issued over the next few years to the Regulars. Note the reinforcing on his trousers and the double-loop ammunition belt that was designed to carry both carbine rounds and pistol rounds (the pistol round loops are empty on the right). (USCM)

Right: By 1899, specifications for enlisted khaki blouses called for a roll collar, as worn by this private who guards two prisoners on punishment duty. His 1889-pattern campaign hat bears the company and regimental numeral in bronze (also specified by orders in 1899). He wears khaki trousers rather than khaki breeches, despite the fact that he is a cavalryman. The prisoner on the right wears the brown canvas suit adopted by General Orders No. 32, 16 April 1884. The other prisoner has obtained a non-regulation belt to hold up his brown canvas work trousers and wears a short-sleeved wool/cotton knit undershirt. (UK)

Opposite page, top left: Cavalry colonels, such as C. C. C. Carr who commanded the Fourth U.S. Cavalry, wore their insignia of rank on the shoulder loops of their 1898-pattern khaki jacket, and the Arms of the United States with the crossed saber insignia on the collars. The hat cord on the 1889-pattern campaign hat is gold and black intermixed, as had been the case for officers' cords since the 1850s. (UK)

Opposite page, top right: From 1900, regimental staff officers and squadron adjutants began to wear their crossed saber insignia with the staff devices below, and the regimental number above. This captain was the quartermaster of the Eighth U.S. Cavalry, and wears the 1895-pattern jacket. (USCM)

Opposite page, bottom: Cavalry first lieutenants through lieutenant colonels wore their rank and the Arms of the United States on the yellow shoulder tabs of their 1898-pattern khaki blouses, and the crossed sabers with regimental number on their collars as shown by these two officers in 1902. (UK)

Below: This photograph, taken at Fort Huachuca, Arizona Territory around 1903, depicts the transition from the 1895-pattern officers' forage cap to the new 1902-pattern dress cap with its slightly 'belled' crown. In 1902, officers were also ordered to replace the 'U.S.' device on the collars of their blouses with a gilt Arms of the United States. As always during periods of uniform change, several variations existed side-by-side. (AHS)

Above: At the end of 1902, the cavalry underwent a major uniform change, although a number of previously issued items remained in use. This private, stationed at Fort Walla Walla, Washington c. 1905, wears the five-button blue wool blouse, among other 19th century items, although he has the new Springfield .30 caliber bolt-action rifle in his rifle scabbard, a weapon which began to replace the Krag after 1903. The bit is the M1892 on the curb bridle. (CBF)

Opposite page, top: These troopers of the Fourteenth Cavalry have used their .30 caliber Springfield rifles accurately on a hunting foray c. 1905. Note the man holding the game has on an 1883-pattern shirt, while the soldier to his right sports a large neckerchief and a civilian-style holster, perhaps manufactured at the Arsenal of Manila. The individual standing second from the right also has goggles around

his hat, a practical accessory bought by some troops to protect the eyes on mounted details. (CBF)

Opposite page, bottom: Some examples of the various uniform changes for enlisted men ushered in by General Order No. 130, 31 December 1902 are evident in this photograph of Fourteenth Cavalry troopers in their barracks. Some of the men wear the old 1883-pattern blue wool shirt, while others have the 1902-pattern olive drab (O.D.) flannel shirt. The soldier on the far left, seated atop the end of his bunk, wears the olive drab service dress. A pair of 1902-pattern campaign hats hang from the back wall. Several men have on olive drab trousers and others kersey blue trousers. Two of the men wear suspenders, an issue item since the mid-1880s, but contrary to the Hollywood image, seldom visible when worn. (CBF)

Opposite page, top: As these men of Troop B, Fourteenth U.S. Cavalry break for chow, they pose in the olive drab wool shirt and breeches with campaign hats, all of the 1902-pattern. Some of the men have procured bandannas, and at least two of them have on the issue woolen O.D. sweater. (CBF)

Opposite page, bottom: The 1902-pattern brown canvas fatigue clothing, consisting of an 8-ounce brown dyed canvas jacket with six black buttons and a pair of canvas overalls, was ideal for heavy work. Here at Fort Walla Walla, Washington's wood supply yard, a steam tractor is employed in providing fuel for the garrison. (CBF)

Right: The 1902 regulation full dress uniform for enlisted men consisted of a dark blue coat with six buttons. The shoulder loops, collar, and cuffs were trimmed in yellow mohair piping. A pair of yellow stripes of facing material were sewn on a blue wool detachable band to be worn on the 'bellcrown' cap, while a worsted yellow breast cord formed another part of the full dress or parade kit. Also seen are the 1902-pattern buckskin gauntlets, an M1902 saber belt, and light blue kersey trousers for dismounted wear. (CBF)

Above: By removing the hat band and breast cord, the full dress enlisted uniform prescribed at the end of 1902 by General Order No. 30 could be converted to the dress uniform for enlisted men. The collar and cap insignia remained the same, as did the coat, white Berlin gloves, and sky-blue kersey trousers. Note the service stripes on the lower sleeves that indicated the completion of one enlistment of 'faithful' service. (CBF)

Above right: For mounted wear with the full dress and dress uniforms, enlisted men were authorized the olive drab wool service breeches. By 1907, however, the sky-blue trousers were to be combined with the full dress coat, and worn with either canvas or leather leggings. (CBF)

B Troop 14 US Cav Fort Walla Walla

Opposite page, bottom right: A trooper of the Fourteenth Cavalry in the olive drab wool enlisted service dress prescribed by the new 1902 regulations and issued over the next few years. The jacket had a roll collar. Chevrons worn points up on the sleeves were to indicate the rank of non-commissioned officers and lance corporals, as seen here. Originally, the stripes were of yellow facing material on olive drab for cavalry, but the facing material was changed to khaki in 1905. (CBF)

Above: Troop B, Fourteenth U.S. Cavalry, forms two ranks in their 1902-pattern olive drab service dress. A khaki version

of the uniform was provided for hot weather and wear in tropical climates, such as the Philippines and Hawaii. This unit was stationed at Fort Walla Walla, Washington (seen in the background) from 1905 through 1908. (CBF)

Below: In this *c.* 1905 image, olive drab-clad troopers at Fort Leavenworth, Kansas participate in a bareback mounted tug-of-war competition during a field day where equestrian skills and physical fitness were tested. Such competitions were typical early in the 20th century as part of the military's effort to maintain a combat-ready force. (FAM)

Left: Olive drab was introduced with the uniform adopted by General Order No. 130, 30 December 1902. This trooper of the Fourteenth U.S. Cavalry wears the 1902-pattern flannel O.D. shirt, with O.D. service breeches held up by a russet leather belt. His headgear is the 1902-pattern campaign hat. Note also that canvas leggings have replaced leather boots for cavalry enlisted men. The pistol cartridge belt with loops on the left side may have been made at the Maestranza de Manila (Arsenal of Manila) in the Philippines, a facility that the U.S. government acquired after the Spanish-American War. This method of carrying pistol ammunition differed from the normal use of russet leather pistol cartridge boxes. (CBF)

Above: Training horses for combat also was a primary goal for cavalrymen, as this trooper of the Fourteenth U.S. Cavalry demonstrates around 1905. Mounts were to be conditioned so they would lie down on command in order to provide cover for their rider during a fight. Note the trooper wears a butt backwards civilian style holster rig, rather than the butt forward cross-draw holster with flap, issued to troops for the .38 caliber Colt revolver. Once again, this may have been an item fabricated at the Arsenal of Manila. (CBF)

Below: Men of the Fourteenth U.S. Cavalry put their horses through their paces, dismounting and bringing the animals down in a circle to form a protective barrier. They wear the 1902-pattern olive drab service uniform. (CBF)

THE SPIRAL
FORT WALLA WALLA WN

Above: Maintaining intervals, even at the gallop, required horses and riders to be in top form, as men from the Fourteenth U.S. Cavalry clearly show in this 'spiral' formation at Fort Walla Walla, Washington *c.* 1905. The men are in the 1902-pattern olive drab service uniform. (CBF)

Below: Wearing the 1902-pattern dress uniform, enlisted men and officers of the Eleventh Cavalry gather for a parade. This picture was taken around 1913. (GH)

Right: Bandsmen, such as Musician William H. Green from the Ninth Cavalry band at Fort Riley, Kansas, had the same uniform as the other ranks for dress and full dress, according to the 1902 regulations, but exchanged crossed sabers for a lyre as insignia. Bandsmen continued to display the double ½-inch stripes of yellow facing material on their trousers. The boots are not regulation, however, and may be a photographer's prop, because shoes had been adopted with canvas or leather leggings with this uniform. The trousers are sky-blue. (UK)

Left: In 1912 the full dress hat with mohair band replaced the dress hat, as seen here in the case of Colonel James Parker, commander of the Eleventh U.S. Cavalry. Parker's cap has gold embroidered oak leaves on the black visor to mark him as a field grade officer. The band of the cap is yellow with gold bullion stripes on either side. Black mohair trims the 1902-pattern dress jacket with its concealed buttons. Service ribbons appear on the chest, having been introduced for that purpose in 1907. The breeches are light blue with 1½-inch leg stripes. (GH)

Above: The M1912 horse equipment was European-inspired. Innovative features included the method of slinging the 1903 Springfield rifle to the waist when mounted, with the butt of the stock resting in a bucket. Although issued to some troops on the 1916 Punitive Expedition on the Mexican-American Border, this experiment did not replace the McClellan saddle that had been in use extensively since the Civil War and remained the standard until the disbandment of the U.S. Cavalry as a horse mounted organization. This man wears the 1905-pattern chevrons of a troop quartermaster sergeant on his 1911-pattern olive drab shirt, which could be worn in the field and for similar duties in place of the service coat, according to the 1912 Uniform Regulations. (RK)

Above: Officers of Troops D and L, First U.S. Cavalry, along with an officer from an improvised field artillery at Calexico, California, near the border with Mexico in 1914. The 1911-pattern olive drab shirt with rank insignia on the collar and 1912-pattern campaign hat are worn by all. (NA)

Right: Private Fingarden of Troop A, Fifth U.S. Cavalry, is mounted with the 1904 russet cavalry equipment that was more commonly provided during the Punitive Expedition of 1916. Note the 'U.S.' embossed on the hood of his right stirrup. He also has the M1914 bandoleer and the M1907 canvas leggings. (NA)

Left: The 1911-pattern olive drab service coat (not actually issued until 1912 or thereafter) had a stand collar and was to bear circular disks instead of crossed sabers as insignia on the collar. The bronze disks had screwbacks and measured 1-inch in diameter, the one on the left side bearing crossed sabers with the regimental numeral and company letter where applicable, while the one on the right was to display a 'U.S.' As of 30 December 1916 these insignia could be worn on the shirt if the coat was not worn. This trooper has slung the M1914 cavalry bandoleer across from his shoulder to hip, and has the M1912 mounted pistol holster and M1912 horse equipment. (RK)

Left: Two men from Troop E, Fifth U.S. Cavalry, wear 1911-pattern shirts and breeches, and the 1912-pattern 'Montana' peak campaign hat with yellow worsted hat cords that terminated in acorns. The leather puttees appear to be the M1907 type, and the holsters are the M1912 pattern with swivels for mounted troops. (NA)

Below: Leather chinstraps were one means used to secure the campaign hat as Privates Hart and Shicosky, Troop C Fifth U.S. Cavalry, did in 1916 while pursuing 'Pancho' Villa. (NA)

Right: The 1904 horse equipment included a russet leather scabbard to carry the .30 caliber Springfield rifle on the right forward side of the horse when mounted, as Private Lewis, Troop C, Fifth U.S. Cavalry, would have done in 1916. (NA)

Above: At Dublan, Mexico on 17 April 1916 troopers buy items to supplement their issue from the army. They appear in both M1910 leather and canvas versions of the leggings, while two of the men have obtained goggles that were practical protection against dust, although not provided by the government. The man in the center forefront has a leg strap to keep his M1912 holster in place, while the man on the far right has removed his canteen from his carrier on his left hip, perhaps to buy something besides water as a refill. The same individual has a leather field glasses case. (NA)

Below: Troop C, Fifth U.S. Cavalry's Private Fitzgerald wears the summer undershirt, 1911-pattern olive drab breeches, held up by the russet leather garrison belt, and the ubiquitous 1912-pattern 'hat, service, olive drab.' (NA)

Right: Private Shanger's mount at El Valle, Mexico, during September 1916 has a 'U.S.' brand on his left shoulder as identification that this horse belonged to 'Uncle Sam.' Shanger's leather hat chin strap was not common, shoestrings being more typical. His canvas leggings were also of an unusual type. (NA)

Left: Private Bocke, Troop C, Fifth U.S. Cavalry at El Valle, Mexico was photographed on 18 September 1916, in his privately purchased leather boots with combined laces and straps, the 1912-pattern campaign hat, O.D. breeches with 1902-pattern shirt (these had no pocket flaps), both of wool, and the M1910 first aid pouch at his waist on the left hip. The blanket is the M1908, and the horse equipment the M1904 without curb bit. (NA)

Above: Members of Troop C, Fifth U.S. Cavalry, display a number of typical new and old pattern items during 1916, including the russet M1896 saddle that was adopted in 1904. The man posing left of center is a sergeant with the 1905-pattern khaki stripes sewn onto an O.D. backing that in turn was stitched points up to his 1911-pattern shirt. The man at center right wears the 1911-pattern sweater. (NA)

Below: An M1908 blanket covers the McClellan saddle on the left, while a poncho has been draped over the center saddle by these men from Troop C, Fifth U.S. Cavalry in Mexico, 1916. A white undershirt is evident on the trooper at the far right. (NA)

Above: A troop of the Eleventh U.S. Cavalry trailing Villistas through the rugged terrain and challenging climate of the Mexican desert in 1916. (NA)

Below: Apache Indian scouts were among Brigadier General John J. 'Black Jack' Pershing's forces during the Punitive Expedition. The employment of these men in this foray into Mexico would be the closing chapter in this unit's history and the history of the horse soldier in the United States Army in terms of actual field operations. (NA)

INDEX

Adjutant/Aide de Camp, 36, 51
African–American/Black/Colored Troops/Negro, 36
Aiguillette, 36
Allied Expeditionary Force (AEF), 8
Apache, 5–6, 38, 72
Arms of the United States/Coat of Arms (Insignia), 9, 51
Arsenal of Manila/Maestranza Manila, 52, 58–9
Artillery, 12, 15, 64

Baker and McKenney, 25
Band, 2, 36–37, 60
Bandanna/Neckerchief/Kerchief, 26, 52, 55
Bandoleer, 65
Belt, 26, 58, 68
   Buckle/Plate, 9
   Pistol, 58
   Saber, 47, 55
Bit, 44, 47, 52, 70
Blanket, 70–71
Blouse
   Enlisted, 1872-pattern, 26–27
   Enlisted, 1874-pattern, 27, 29
   Enlisted, 1884-pattern, 13–14, 29, 34, 41, 43, 47, 52
   Khaki, 16, 48, 51
   Officer, 1872-pattern, 21–2
   Officer, 1875-pattern, 35
   Officer, 1895-pattern, 44, 47, 51
   Officer, 1895-pattern (Summer), 44
   Officer, 1902-pattern, Dress (Jacket), 51, 63
Bocke, Private, 70
Boehm, First Lieutenant Peter, 25
Boots, 20, 29, 38, 44, 58, 60, 70
"Boots and Saddles," 8
Boughton, Lieutenant Daniel, 31
Boxer Rebellion, 7
Brand, 69
Breast Cord, 55–6
Breeches (see also Jodhpurs), 48, 55–56, 58, 63, 66, 68
Bridle, 6, 45, 52
Brown, Lieutenant L.C., 38
Buckskin, 20
Bugler/Trumpeter, 2, 9, 15–16, 36
Bunk, 52
Button, 18, 21, 47, 54

Calexico, California, 64
Canada, 5
Canteen, 68
Cap
   Forage/"Bummer's"/1857-pattern, 17
   Forage, Chasseur, 17, 19–20
   Forage, Cord/Strap, 31
   Forage, 1872-pattern, 14, 22–23, 26–27, 31, 34–35, 37, 41
   Forage, 1895-pattern, 36, 43, 47–8, 51
   "McDowell," 2
   Muskrat/Fur (Hat), 29, 35
   1902-pattern Full Dress/Dress, 51, 55–56, 63
Cape/Cloak, 44
Carbine
   Boot, 38
   Krag-Jörgensen .30-40 caliber, 7, 47–8, 51
   Sling, 38
   Springfield .45-70 (Trapdoor), 7, 29, 38
Carr, Colonel C.C.C., 51
Cartridge/Ammunition
   Belt, 29, 48
   Pouch, 58
Cavalry, passim
   and Light Artillery School, 41, 43
   School of Application for Infantry and Cavalry, 6
   First U.S., 7, 37–9, 64
   First Volunteer/"Rough Riders," 7
   Second U.S., 7, 43–45, 47
   Third U.S., 7, 22, 31, 37, 41
   Fourth U.S., 25, 51
   Fifth U.S., 44, 48, 65–8, 70–71
   Sixth U.S., 7, 27
   Seventh U.S., 8, 20, 23–4, 26–7, 35, 37
   Eighth U.S., 7, 51
   Ninth U.S., 6–7, 60
   Tenth U.S., 6–7, 18, 31, 36
   Eleventh U.S./Eleventh Armored (Black Horse), 7, 60, 63, 72
   Eleventh U.S. Volunteers, 7
   Fourteenth U.S., 43, 47, 52, 55, 57–60
   Fifteenth U.S., 7
Chaplain, 6
Chevrons/Non-commissioned Rank Insignia/Stripes
   Coat and Jacket, 14, 17, 37, 41, 57
   Overcoat, 44
   Service, 12, 56
   Shirt, 63, 71
Cheyenne, 6–7
China, 7
Civil War, 45, 63
Coat
   Frock, Company Grade, 20
   Full Dress/Dress, Enlisted 1902-pattern, 55–6, 60
   Mounted, Dress, 1872-pattern, 23, 32
   Mounted, Dress, 1885-pattern, 35–7
   Mounted, Dress, 1887-pattern, 12, 35
   Musician, 2, 32

Officer's 1872-pattern, Dress, 25
Officer's 1880-pattern, Dress, 15, 25, 31
Service, 1902-pattern, 57
Service, 1911-pattern (aka M1911), 65
Service, 1912-pattern (aka M1912), 63, 65
Columbus, NM, 8
Comanche, 5
Cravat, 34
Crook, Brigadier General George, 15
Crow, 6–7, 37
Cuba, 7, 16
Custer, Major General George, 5, 20

Dinwiddie Courthouse, VA, 25
Donnelly, Private Timothy, 26
Dublan, Mexico, 68

El Valle, Mexico, 69-70
Evans, Private, 47

Farrier, 13
Fatigue Clothing (See Also Coveralls), 48, 55
Fenians, 5
Field
   Glasses/Binoculars, 68
Fingarden, Private, 65
First-Aid
   Pouch/Kit, 71
Fitzgerald, Private, 68
Fort Abraham Lincoln, ND, 24
Fort Bridger, WY, 21
Fort Ethan Allen, VT, 6
Fort Leavenworth, KS, 6, 57
Fort Myer, VA, 6
Fort Riley, KS, 6, 32, 41, 43, 47, 60
Fort Sumter, SC, 5
Fort Walla Walla, WA, 52, 55, 57, 60
Fort Washakie, WY, 39
Fort Wingate, NM, 36

"Galvanized Yankees," 5
Gauntlets, 17, 47, 55
Gloves
   Berlin, 56
Goggles, 52, 68
Green, Musician William, 60
Guerrero, Mexico, 8
Guidon, 32, 38

Hart, Private, 66
Hat
   Campaign, 1872-pattern (folding), 21, 26–7
   Campaign, 1883-pattern, 39
   Campaign, 1889-pattern, 35, 39, 45, 47–48, 51
   Campaign, 1902/03-pattern, 52, 55, 58
   Campaign, 1911/1912-pattern (AKA "Montana Peak"
      and "Smokey the Bear"), 64, 66, 68, 70
   Cords, 9, 11, 27, 51, 66
   1858-pattern (AKA "Hardee" or "Jeff Davis"), 2, 9, 11
   Slouch, 20, 27, 35
   Strap, 66, 69
Hawaii, 7, 57

Helmet
   Cord, 23–25, 31–32
   Mounted, 1872-pattern, 23–25
   Mounted, 1881-pattern, 15, 31–32, 35
   Summer, 43, 47
Herringbone/Herring-bone, 37
Holster, 52, 58–9, 65–6, 68, 70
Horse Equipment, 44, 63, 65, 67
Horse-holder, 6

Indian Scout, 6, 72
Infantry, 6
Insignia
   Cap/Hat, 2, 9, 11, 17, 27, 31, 34, 48, 56, 60
   Cavalry, 2, 9, 11, 17, 27, 31, 44, 51, 60, 65
   Collar/Lapel, 23, 32, 35, 44, 47, 51, 56, 85
   Helmet, 25, 31
   Marksmanship/Shooting, 34, 41
   Musician/Band, 60
   Rank/Specialty, 13, 64

Jacket
   Enlisted, Mounted, 1854/55-pattern, 9, 17–18
Jefferson Barracks, MO, 37
Jefferson, Private John, 36
Junction City, KS, 43

Kersey, 18, 21, 43, 52, 55–6
Kiowa, 5
Knots
   Shoulder, 12, 25

La Guasima, Cuba, 7
Lakota/Sioux, 6–7
Lava Beds, 5
Leggings, 38, 37, 56, 58, 60, 65, 68–9
Lewis, Private, 67
Little Bighorn, 5

Mauser, 7
Maxon, Captain M.M., 31
Maximilian, Emperor, 5
Mess
   Hall, 41
Mexican
   Border, 63–64
Mexico, 5, 72
Mississippi River, 5
Modoc, 5
Musician, 60

National Park, 5
Nez Perce, 5

Ogden, H.A., 16
Ogden, Private John S., 24
Olive Drab (OD), 8, 52, 55–60, 63–64, 68, 70–71
Overalls, 12, 43
Overcoat (Greatcoat)
   Enlisted, 11, 21
   Officer, 19, 31, 44
Overshoes (Arctic), 29

Panama, 7
Parker, Colonel James, 63
Peking, 7
Pennell, Joseph, 43
Pershing, General John J. "Black Jack," 8, 72
Philippines, 7, 16, 57
Pistol, 39, 58–9
Plume, 15, 23, 25
Pole, Musician Clarence, 36
Poncho, 71
Puerto Rico, 7, 16
Punitive Expedition, 8, 63, 65, 72
Puttees, 66

Quartermaster, 11, 63

Ribbons, 63
Rifle
    Springfield .30 caliber, 52, 63, 67
Riley, Private William E., 39
Russell, Second Lieutenant A.H., 22
Russell, Lieutenant G.M., 47

Saber, 8, 21, 25
    Cavalry, Officer, M187, 31, 44
    Light Cavalry, M1859, 21, 37–38
Sack Coat, four-button, 19–20
Saddle
    Bags, 44
    Cloth, 47
    McClellan, 43–44, 63, 71
San Carlos Agency, AZ, 38
San Juan Hill, 7
Scabbard/Bucket, Carbine/Rifle/Submachine Gun, 63, 67
Scanton, Private C.M., 32
Scarf, 20
Shanger, Private, 69
Shicosky, Private, 66
Shirt
    1874-pattern, 26
    1875-pattern, 29
    1877-pattern, 29
    1881-pattern, 27
    1883-pattern, 29, 43, 47, 52
    1902-pattern, Chambray, 41, 58

1902/1904-pattern, 53, 70
1910/11-pattern, 63–4, 66, 71
Non-regulation, 18, 34
Shoes, 60
Shotgun/Forage Gun, 29
Shoulder
    Knot, 12, 36–37
    Strap, 21–22, 35
Spanish–American War, 16
Squires, Second Lieutenant H.G., 25
Stable Frock, 12, 39, 44–45
Steam Tractor, 55
Stirrup, 65
Suspenders, 18, 47, 52
Sweater, 55, 71

Taylor, Private William O., 23, 27
Trefoil, 21
Trousers/Trowsers
    Fatigue/Work, Brown Canvas, 48, 55
    Field, Olive Drab (Mustard) Wool, 52, 55
    Khaki, 41, 48
    Sky-blue/Blue, 18, 35, 43, 47–48, 52, 55–56, 71
    Stripes/Welt, 14, 17, 20, 35–7, 41, 60, 63
    White Duck/Stable/Summer, 45, 47

Undershirt/Under-Shirt/Underwear, 43, 48, 71
Uniform
    Khaki, 16, 57
    1902-pattern, 16, 57, 59–60
United States
    Military Academy/West Point, NY, 17–18
Upton, Major General Emory, 6

Vest/Waistcoat, 66, 72
Villa, Francisco "Pancho," 8, 66, 72

Walker, Private George, 26
Weaver, Private Howard, 26
Wilson, Woodrow, 8
Wolford, Private C.A., 38
Wounded Knee, SD, 35

Yates, Captain George, 20